How to Read the Bible Every Day

*A One-Year, Two-Year, & Three-Year
Plan for Reading through the Scriptures*

Carmen Rojas

SERVANT BOOKS
Ann Arbor, Michigan

Copyright © 1988 by Servant Publications
All rights reserved.

Published by Servant Books
P.O. Box 8617
Ann Arbor, Michigan 48107

The three Bible reading plans and the supplemental list of
seasonal readings for the church year were drawn up by
Carmen Rojas.

Cover design by Michael P. Andaloro

Printed in the United States of America
ISBN 0-89283-399-8

90 91 92 10 9 8 7 6 5 4

Library of Congress Cataloging-in-Publication Data

How to read the Bible every day.

  1. Bible—Reading. I. Rojas, Carmen.
BS617.H64 1988   220'.07   88-11536
ISBN 0-89283-399-8

Foreword

THE HOLY BIBLE is God's Word addressed to us now, in our own life situation, for our instruction and for our formation in Christ. While the Bible does not give us all the answers we need for living, it does give us inspired guidance and a powerful spirituality. In fact, our friends in Marriage Encounter, a renewal movement in the Chrurch for married couples, tell us that these inspired books are God's love letters to us. How true that is.

The Bible has been described as the Instruction Manual, drawn up by God, for Christian living. That also is true. As some people make the mistake of looking at an instruction manual only after all else has failed, so we creatures can make the mistake of turning to the Bible only after our lives have fallen apart. The right way to live is to read the Bible regularly in order to learn how to live, in order to avoid making mistakes that could lead us into sin.

That is why I have regularly instructed the people of the Archdiocese of Hartford to do daily Bible readings during Lent and Advent. I have also recommended to my people the yearly Bible readings of the American Bible Society. Therefore, I warmly commend this plan of daily Bible readings. Like the rain that comes down from above, may these readings bring the Word of God into your soul. May they nourish your spiritual life with God's abundant blessings.

—The Most Reverend John F. Whealon
Archbishop of Hartford

Introduction

HOW TO READ THE BIBLE EVERY DAY is designed to help Catholics read Scripture daily at their own pace. It includes three reading plans and a supplemental list of seasonal readings for the church year.

The one-year plan, which covers the entire Bible in one year, is ideal for those who are reading Scripture regularly. The daily reading time averages 20-30 minutes. On the other hand, the three-year plan is ideal for those who want to start reading Scripture regularly. The daily reading time averages only 5-7 minutes, and the entire Bible is covered within three years. The two-year reading plan, which is keyed to the church year and covers the entire Bible in two years, is ideally suited for those who want to follow the daily readings of the liturgy. The reading time for this plan averages 10-15 minutes every day.

How to Read the Bible Every Day also includes a list of Scripture readings for the special liturgical seasons of the church year: Advent, Christmas, Lent, and Easter. These seasonal readings can be profitably used with any of the three reading plans.

Readers who use this guide should take note that all of the scriptural references by chapter and verse follow the numbering scheme of the revised edition of the *New American Bible*, including the new translation of the New Testament. The correct numbering of chapters and verses for readings may vary slightly at times if another version of the Bible is used.

Finally, Catholics are expected to use a Bible with an imprimatur in their study of Scripture, preferably one with helpful introductions and footnotes. Both the *New American Bible* and the *Jerusalem Bible*, which include introductions and footnotes, meet these qualifications.

Part One

One-Year Reading Plan

(The Bible in One Year, Old Testament and New Testament Daily Readings)

Daily Reading Time averages 20-30 minutes. This reading plan is particularly suited to those who are already reading Scripture every day.

JANUARY

Date	OT	NT
1	Genesis 1-2	Mark 1:1-13
2	Genesis 3-4	Mark 1:14-28
3	Genesis 5-6	Mark 1:29-39
4	Genesis 7-8	Mark 1:40-45
5	Genesis 9-10	Mark 2:1-12
6	Genesis 11-12	Mark 2:13-17
7	Genesis 13-15	Mark 2:18-28
8	Genesis 16-18	Mark 3:1-12
9	Genesis 19-20	Mark 3:13-35
10	Genesis 21-23	Mark 4:1-25
11	Genesis 24-26	Mark 4:26-34
12	Genesis 27-28	Mark 4:35-41
13	Genesis 29-30	Mark 5:1-20
14	Genesis 31-32	Mark 5:21-43
15	Genesis 33-36	Mark 6:1-13
16	Genesis 37-39	Mark 6:14-29
17	Genesis 40-42	Mark 6:30-56
18	Genesis 43-46	Mark 7:1-23
19	Genesis 47-50	Mark 7:24-37
20	Exodus 1-2	Mark 8:1-26
21	Exodus 3-4	Mark 8:27-9:1
22	Exodus 5-6:27	Mark 9:2-13
23	Exodus 6:28-8	Mark 9:14-29
24	Exodus 9-10	Mark 9:30-50
25	Exodus 11-12	Mark 10:1-16
26	Exodus 13-14	Mark 10:17-34
27	Exodus 15-16	Mark 10:35-52
28	Exodus 17-18	Mark 11:1-14
29	Exodus 19-20	Mark 11:15-33
30	Exodus 21-22	Mark 12:1-17
31	Exodus 23-24	Mark 12:18-34

FEBRUARY

Date	OT	NT
1	Exodus 25-26	Mark 12:35-44
2	Exodus 27-28	Mark 13
3	Exodus 29-30	Mark 14:1-16
4	Exodus 31-32	Mark 14:17-42
5	Exodus 33-34	Mark 14:43-72
6	Exodus 35-36	Mark 15:1-20

Date	OT	NT
7	Exodus 37-38	Mark 15:21-47
8	Exodus 39-40	Mark 16
9	Leviticus 1-3	Romans 1:1-17
10	Leviticus 4-6	Romans 1:18-32
11	Leviticus 7-9	Romans 2:1-16
12	Leviticus 10-12	Romans 2:17-3:20
13	Leviticus 13-14	Romans 3:21-4:25
14	Leviticus 15-16	Romans 5:1-21
15	Leviticus 17-18	Romans 6:1-23
16	Leviticus 19-20	Romans 7
17	Leviticus 21-22	Romans 8:1-27
18	Leviticus 23-24	Romans 8:28-39
19	Leviticus 25-26	Romans 9:1-33
20	Leviticus 27	Romans 10-11
21	Numbers 1-3	Romans 12
22	Numbers 4-5	Romans 13
23	Numbers 6-7	Romans 14
24	Numbers 8-10	Romans 15
25	Numbers 11-14	Romans 16
26	Numbers 15-18	Hebrews 1-2
27	Numbers 19-21	Hebrews 3
28	Numbers 22-24	Hebrews 4:1-13

MARCH

Date	OT	NT
1	Numbers 25-27	Hebrews 4:14-5:10
2	Numbers 28-31	Hebrews 5:11-6:20
3	Numbers 32-34	Hebrews 7
4	Deuteronomy 1-3	Hebrews 8-9:10
5	Deuteronomy 4-5	Hebrews 9:11-10:18
6	Deuteronomy 6-8	Hebrews 10:19-39
7	Deuteronomy 9-11	Hebrews 11
8	Deuteronomy 12-14	Hebrews 12
9	Deuteronomy 15-18	Hebrews 13
10	Deuteronomy 19-23	1 Peter 1:1-12
11	Deuteronomy 24-25	1 Peter 1:13-25
12	Deuteronomy 26-29	1 Peter 2:1-12
13	Deuteronomy 30-32	1 Peter 2:13-25
14	Deuteronomy 33-34	1 Peter 3:1-12
15	Joshua 1-4	1 Peter 3:13-22
16	Joshua 5-9	1 Peter 4:1-11
17	Joshua 10-14	1 Peter 4:12-19

Date	OT	NT
18	Joshua 15-19	1 Peter 5:1-14
19	Joshua 20-24	1 Corinthians 1:1-25
20	Judges 1-2	1 Corinthians 1:26-2:16
21	Judges 3-5	1 Corinthians 3
22	Judges 6-8	1 Corinthians 4
23	Judges 9-12	1 Corinthians 5
24	Judges 13-16	1 Corinthians 6
25	Judges 17-19	1 Corinthians 7:1-24
26	Judges 20-21	1 Corinthians 7:25-40
27	Ruth	1 Corinthians 8
28	1 Samuel 1-2	1 Corinthians 9:1-18
29	1 Samuel 3-4	1 Corinthians 9:19-27
30	1 Samuel 5-7	1 Corinthians 10
31	1 Samuel 8-10	1 Corinthians 11

APRIL

Date	OT	NT
1	1 Samuel 11-14	1 Corinthians 12:1-11
2	1 Samuel 15-17	1 Corinthians 12:12-31
3	1 Samuel 18-21:1	1 Corinthians 13
4	1 Samuel 21:2-25:43	1 Corinthians 14
5	1 Samuel 26-31	1 Corinthians 15
6	2 Samuel 1-3	1 Corinthians 16
7	2 Samuel 4-7	Matthew 1:1-17
8	2 Samuel 8-10	Matthew 1:18-25
9	2 Samuel 11-13	Matthew 2:1-12
10	2 Samuel 14-16	Matthew 2:13-23
11	2 Samuel 17-19	Matthew 3:1-12
12	2 Samuel 20-22	Matthew 3:13-17
13	2 Samuel 23-24	Matthew 4:1-11
14	1 Kings 1-3	Matthew 4:12-17
15	1 Kings 4-6	Matthew 4:18-25
16	1 Kings 7-9	Matthew 5:1-16
17	1 Kings 10-12	Matthew 5:17-30
18	1 Kings 13-15	Matthew 5:31-48
19	1 Kings 16-18	Matthew 6:1-16
20	1 Kings 19-22	Matthew 6:17-33
21	2 Kings 1-3	Matthew 7:1-23
22	2 Kings 4-6:23	Matthew 7:24-29
23	2 Kings 6:24-7:20	Matthew 8:1-22
24	2 Kings 8-10	Matthew 8:23-9:8
25	2 Kings 11-12	Matthew 9:9-13

Date	OT	NT
26	2 Kings 13-15	Matthew 9:14-17
27	2 Kings 16-18	Matthew 9:18-26
28	2 Kings 19-20	Matthew 9:27-34
29	2 Kings 21-23	Matthew 9:35-11:1
30	2 Kings 24-25	Matthew 11:2-24

MAY

Date	OT	NT
1	1 Chronicles 1-3	Matthew 11:25-30
2	1 Chronicles 4-6	Matthew 12:1-21
3	1 Chronicles 7-9:34	Matthew 12:22-37
4	1 Chronicles 9:35-12:41	Matthew 12:38-45
5	1 Chronicles 13-16	Matthew 12:46-50
6	1 Chronicles 17-20	Matthew 13:1-23
7	1 Chronicles 21-24	Matthew 13:24-43
8	1 Chronicles 25-29	Matthew 13:44-53
9	2 Chronicles 1-4	Matthew 13:54-58
10	2 Chronicles 5-7	Matthew 14:1-12
11	2 Chronicles 8-10	Matthew 14:13-21
12	2 Chronicles 11-14	Matthew 14:22-36
13	2 Chronicles 15-19	Matthew 15:1-20
14	2 Chronicles 20-24	Matthew 15:21-31
15	2 Chronicles 25-28	Matthew 15:32-39
16	2 Chronicles 29-32	Matthew 16:1-12
17	2 Chronicles 33-36	Matthew 16:13-20
18	Ezra 1-3	Matthew 16:21-28
19	Ezra 4-6	Matthew 17:1-13
20	Ezra 7-10	Matthew 17:14-21
21	Nehemiah 1-3	Matthew 17:22-27
22	Nehemiah 4-6	Matthew 18:1-9
23	Nehemiah 7-9	Matthew 18:10-18
24	Nehemiah 10-13	Matthew 18:19-35
25	Tobit 1-3	Matthew 19:1-12
26	Tobit 4-6	Matthew 19:13-30
27	Tobit 7-9	Matthew 20:1-16
28	Tobit 10-14	Matthew 20:17-28
29	Judith 1-3	Matthew 20:29-34
30	Judith 4-6	Matthew 21:1-11
31	Judith 7-9	Matthew 21:12-17

JUNE

Date	OT	NT
1	Judith 10-13	Matthew 21:18-27
2	Judith 14-16	Matthew 21:28-46
3	Esther A, 1-3, B	Matthew 22:1-14
4	Esther 4, C, D, 5	Matthew 22:15-22
5	Esther 6, 7, 8, E	Matthew 22:23-33
6	Esther (8), 9, F	Matthew 22:34-46
7	1 Maccabees 1-2	Matthew 23:1-12
8	1 Maccabees 3-5	Matthew 23:13-23
9	1 Maccabees 6-9	Matthew 23:24-39
10	1 Maccabees 10-13	Matthew 24:1-14
11	1 Maccabees 14-16	Matthew 24:15-25
12	2 Maccabees 1-2	Matthew 24:26-51
13	2 Maccabees 3-4	Matthew 25:1-13
14	2 Maccabees 5-6	Matthew 25:14-30
15	2 Maccabees 7-8	Matthew 25:31-46
16	2 Maccabees 9-11	Matthew 26:1-19
17	2 Maccabees 12-13	Matthew 26:20-46
18	2 Maccabees 14-15	Matthew 26:47-75
19	Job 1-3	Matthew 27:1-31
20	Job 4-7	Matthew 27:32-66
21	Job 8-10	Matthew 28
22	Job 11-14	1 Timothy 1
23	Job 15-17	1 Timothy 2
24	Job 18-21	1 Timothy 3
25	Job 22-24	1 Timothy 4
26	Job 25-28	1 Timothy 5
27	Job 29-31	1 Timothy 6
28	Job 32-34	Titus 1
29	Job 35-37	Titus 2
30	Job 38-42	Titus 3

JULY

Date	OT	NT
1	Psalms 1-5	2 Corinthians 1:1-2:4
2	Psalms 6-10	2 Corinthians 2:5-17
3	Psalms 11-15	2 Corinthians 3
4	Psalms 16-20	2 Corinthians 4:1-15
5	Psalms 21-25	2 Corinthians 4:16-5:10
6	Psalms 26-30	2 Corinthians 5:11-21

Date	OT	NT
7	Psalms 31-35	2 Corinthians 6:1-7:1
8	Psalms 36-39	2 Corinthians 7:2-16
9	Psalms 40-44	2 Corinthians 8
10	Psalms 45-49	2 Corinthians 9
11	Psalms 50-54	2 Corinthians 10
12	Psalms 55-60	2 Corinthians 11:1-15
13	Psalms 61-66	2 Corinthians 11:16-33
14	Psalms 67-70	2 Corinthians 12:1-10
15	Psalms 71-75	2 Corinthians 12:11-13:13
16	Psalms 76-79	John 1:1-18
17	Psalms 80-84	John 1:19-51
18	Psalms 85-89	John 2
19	Psalms 90-96	John 3:1-21
20	Psalms 97-102	John 3:22-36
21	Psalms 103-106	John 4:1-42
22	Psalms 107-111	John 4:43-5:15
23	Psalms 112-118	John 5:16-30
24	Psalms 119	John 5:31-47
25	Psalms 120-127	John 6:1-24
26	Psalms 128-136	John 6:25-59
27	Psalms 137-141	John 6:60-71
28	Psalms 142-145	John 7:1-13
29	Psalms 146-150	John 7:14-36
30	Proverbs 1-4	John 7:37-52
31	Proverbs 5-8	John 7:53-8:1-11

AUGUST

Date	OT	NT
1	Proverbs 9-12	John 8:12-30
2	Proverbs 13-15	John 8:31-59
3	Proverbs 16-18	John 9
4	Proverbs 19-21	John 10:1-21
5	Proverbs 22-24	John 10:22-42
6	Proverbs 25-27	John 11:1-44
7	Proverbs 28-31	John 11:45-57
8	Ecclesiastes 1-3	John 12:1-19
9	Ecclesiastes 4-9	John 12:20-50
10	Ecclesiastes 10-12	John 13:1-17
11	Song of Songs 1-4	John 13:18-38
12	Song of Songs 5-8	John 14:1-21
13	Wisdom 1-4:19	John 14:22-31
14	Wisdom 4:20-8:1-21	John 15:1-17

Date	OT	NT
15	Wisdom 9-12	John 15:18-27
16	Wisdom 13-16	John 16:1-16
17	Wisdom 17-19	John 16:17-33
18	Sirach 1-3:28	John 17:1-19
19	Sirach 3:29-6:37	John 17:20-26
20	Sirach 7-10	John 18:1-27
21	Sirach 11-14:2	John 18:28-19:16
22	Sirach 14:3-18:33	John 19:17-42
23	Sirach 19-22	John 20:1-18
24	Sirach 23-25	John 20:19-31
25	Sirach 26-29	John 21
26	Sirach 30-33	Acts 1-2
27	Sirach 34-36	Acts 3
28	Sirach 37-39	Acts 4
29	Sirach 40-42	Acts 5
30	Sirach 43-44	Acts 6-7
31	Sirach 45-46	Acts 8

SEPTEMBER

Date	OT	NT
1	Sirach 47-49	Acts 9
2	Sirach 50-51	Acts 10
3	Isaiah 1-2	Acts 11
4	Isaiah 3-4	Acts 12
5	Isaiah 5-6	Acts 13
6	Isaiah 7-8	Acts 14
7	Isaiah 9-10	Acts 15
8	Isaiah 11-12	Acts 16
9	Isaiah 13-14	Acts 17
10	Isaiah 15-16	Acts 18
11	Isaiah 17-18	Acts 19
12	Isaiah 19-20	Acts 20
13	Isaiah 21-22	Acts 21
14	Isaiah 23-24	Acts 22:1-29
15	Isaiah 25-26:19	Acts 22:30-23:35
16	Isaiah 26:20-28:29	Acts 24
17	Isaiah 29-30	Acts 25-26
18	Isaiah 31-32	Acts 27
19	Isaiah 33-34	Acts 28
20	Isaiah 35-36	Galatians 1
21	Isaiah 37-39	Galatians 2
22	Isaiah 40-41	Galatians 3

Date	OT	NT
23	Isaiah 42-43	Galatians 4
24	Isaiah 44-45	Galatians 5
25	Isaiah 46-47	Galatians 6
26	Isaiah 48-49	Philippians 1
27	Isaiah 50-51	Philippians 2
28	Isaiah 52-53	Philippians 3
29	Isaiah 54-55	Philippians 4
30	Isaiah 56-57	Jude

OCTOBER

Date	OT	NT
1	Isaiah 58-59	Ephesians 1
2	Isaiah 60-61	Ephesians 2
3	Isaiah 62-63	Ephesians 3
4	Isaiah 64-66	Ephesians 4
5	Jeremiah 1-2	Ephesians 5
6	Jeremiah 3-4	Ephesians 6
7	Jeremiah 5-6	1 Thessalonians 1
8	Jeremiah 7-8	1 Thessalonians 2
9	Jeremiah 9-10	1 Thessalonians 3
10	Jeremiah 11-12	1 Thessalonians 4
11	Jeremiah 13-14	1 Thessalonians 5
12	Jeremiah 15-16	Colossians 1
13	Jeremiah 17-18	Colossians 2
14	Jeremiah 19-20	Colossians 3
15	Jeremiah 21-22	Colossians 4
16	Jeremiah 23-24	1 Timothy 1
17	Jeremiah 25-26	1 Timothy 2
18	Jeremiah 27-28	1 Timothy 3
19	Jeremiah 29-30	1 Timothy 4
20	Jeremiah 31-32	1 Timothy 5
21	Jeremiah 33-34	1 Timothy 6
22	Jeremiah 35-36	2 Peter 1
23	Jeremiah 37-38	2 Peter 2
24	Jeremiah 39-40	2 Peter 3
25	Jeremiah 41-42	2 Thessalonians 1
26	Jeremiah 43-44	2 Thessalonians 2-3
27	Jeremiah 45-46	2 Timothy 1
28	Jeremiah 47-48	2 Timothy 2
29	Jeremiah 49-50	2 Timothy 3
30	Jeremiah 51-52	2 Timothy 4
31	Lamentations 1-2	Philemon

NOVEMBER

Date	OT	NT
1	Lamentations 3-5	Titus
2	Baruch 1-2	James 1
3	Baruch 3-4	James 2
4	Baruch 5-6	James 3
5	Ezekiel 1-3	James 4
6	Ezekiel 4-5	James 5
7	Ezekiel 6-7	1 John 1-3
8	Ezekiel 8-9	1 John 4-5
9	Ezekiel 10-11	2 John
10	Ezekiel 12-13	3 John
11	Ezekiel 14-15	Luke 1-2
12	Ezekiel 16-17	Luke 3
13	Ezekiel 18-19	Luke 4
14	Ezekiel 20-21	Luke 5
15	Ezekiel 22-23	Luke 6
16	Ezekiel 24-25	Luke 7
17	Ezekiel 26-27	Luke 8
18	Ezekiel 28-29	Luke 9
19	Ezekiel 30-31	Luke 10
20	Ezekiel 32-33	Luke 11
21	Ezekiel 34-35	Luke 12
22	Ezekiel 36-37	Luke 13
23	Ezekiel 38-39	Luke 14
24	Ezekiel 40-41	Luke 15
25	Ezekiel 42-43	Luke 16
26	Ezekiel 44-45	Luke 17
27	Ezekiel 46-48	Luke 18
28	Daniel 1-2	Luke 19
29	Daniel 3	Luke 20
30	Daniel 4	Luke 21

DECEMBER

Date	OT	NT
1	Daniel 5-6	Luke 22
2	Daniel 7-8	Luke 23
3	Daniel 9-12	Luke 24
4	Daniel 13-14	Revelation 1
5	Hosea 1-2	Revelation 2:1-11
6	Hosea 3-4	Revelation 2:12-29
7	Hosea 5-6	Revelation 3:1-13

Date	OT	NT
8	Hosea 7-8	Revelation 3:14-22
9	Hosea 9-10	Revelation 4
10	Hosea 11-12	Revelation 5:1-10
11	Hosea 13-14	Revelation 5:11-14
12	Joel 1-2	Revelation 6
13	Joel 3-4	Revelation 7:1-8
14	Amos 1-2	Revelation 7:9-17
15	Amos 3-4	Revelation 8:1-5
16	Amos 5-6	Revelation 8:6-13
17	Amos 7-9	Revelation 9:1-11
18	Obadiah	Revelation 9:12-21
19	Jonah	Revelation 10
20	Micah 1-3	Revelation 11
21	Micah 4-7	Revelation 12
22	Nahum	Revelation 13
23	Habakkuk	Revelation 14
24	Zephaniah	Revelation 15
25	Haggai	Revelation 16
26	Zechariah 1-3	Revelation 17
27	Zechariah 4-6	Revelation 18
28	Zechariah 7-9	Revelation 19
29	Zechariah 10-12	Revelation 20
30	Zechariah 13-14	Revelation 21
31	Malachi	Revelation 22

Part Two

The Two-Year Reading Plan

(The Bible in Two Years. As much as possible, this two-year plan follows the daily readings of the liturgy.)

Daily Reading Time averages 10-15 minutes. This reading plan is particularly suited to those who want to follow the daily readings of the liturgy during the church year.

JANUARY

Date	Year 1	Year 2
1	Mark 1	1 Samuel 1-2
2	Mark 2	1 Samuel 3-4
3	Mark 3	1 Samuel 5-6
4	Mark 4	1 Samuel 7-8
5	Mark 5	1 Samuel 9-10
6	Mark 6	1 Samuel 11-12
7	Mark 7	1 Samuel 13-14
8	Mark 8	1 Samuel 15-16
9	Mark 9	1 Samuel 17-18
10	Mark 10	1 Samuel 19-20
11	Mark 11	1 Samuel 21-22
12	Mark 12	1 Samuel 23-24
13	Mark 13	1 Samuel 25-26
14	Mark 14	1 Samuel 27-28
15	Mark 15	1 Samuel 29-30
16	Mark 16	1 Samuel 31
17	1 John 1-2	2 Samuel 1-2
18	1 John 3-4	2 Samuel 3-4
19	1 John 5	2 Samuel 5-6
20	2 John	2 Samuel 7-8
21	3 John	2 Samuel 9-10
22	Hebrews 1	2 Samuel 11-12
23	Hebrews 2	2 Samuel 13-14
24	Hebrews 3	2 Samuel 15-16
25	Hebrews 4	2 Samuel 17-18
26	Hebrews 5	2 Samuel 19-20
27	Hebrews 6	2 Samuel 21-22
28	Hebrews 7	2 Samuel 23-24
29	Hebrews 8	1 Kings 1-2
30	Hebrews 9:1-14	1 Kings 3
31	Hebrews 9:15-28	1 Kings 4

FEBRUARY

Date	Year 1	Year 2
1	Hebrews 10	1 Kings 5-6
2	Hebrews 11	1 Kings 7-8
3	Hebrews 12	1 Kings 9-10
4	Hebrews 13	1 Kings 11-12
5	Genesis 1-2	1 Kings 13-14
6	Genesis 3-4	1 Kings 15-16

Date	Year 1	Year 2
7	Genesis 5-6	1 Kings 17-18
8	Genesis 7-8	1 Kings 19-20
9	Genesis 9-10	1 Kings 21-22
10	Genesis 11-12	2 Kings 1-2
11	Genesis 13-14	2 Kings 3-4
12	Genesis 15-16	2 Kings 5-6
13	Genesis 17-18	2 Kings 7-8
14	Genesis 19-20	2 Kings 9-10
15	Genesis 21-22	2 Kings 11-12
16	Genesis 23-24	2 Kings 13-14
17	Genesis 25-26	2 Kings 15-16
18	Genesis 27-28	2 Kings 17-18
19	Genesis 29-30	2 Kings 19-20
20	Genesis 31-32	2 Kings 21-22
21	Genesis 33-34	2 Kings 23-24
22	Genesis 35-36	2 Kings 25
23	Genesis 37-38	James 1
24	Genesis 39-40	James 2
25	Genesis 41-42	James 3
26	Genesis 43-44	James 4
27	Genesis 45-46	James 5
28	Genesis 47-48	1 Peter 1

MARCH

Date	Year 1	Year 2
1	Genesis 49-50	1 Peter 2-3
2	Sirach 1-2	1 Peter 4
3	Sirach 3-4	1 Peter 5
4	Sirach 5-6	2 Peter 1
5	Sirach 7-8	2 Peter 2
6	Sirach 9-10	2 Peter 3
7	Sirach 11-12	Ecclesiastes 1-2
8	Sirach 13-14	Ecclesiastes 3-4
9	Sirach 15-16	Ecclesiastes 5-6
10	Sirach 17-18	Ecclesiastes 7-8
11	Sirach 19-20	Ecclesiastes 9-10
12	Sirach 21-22	Ecclesiastes 11-12
13	Sirach 23-24	2 Timothy 1
14	Sirach 25-26	2 Timothy 2
15	Sirach 27-28	2 Timothy 3
16	Sirach 29-30	2 Timothy 4
17	Sirach 31-32	Lamentations 1-2

Date	Year 1	Year 2
18	Sirach 33-34	Lamentations 3-4
19	Sirach 35-36	Lamentations 5
20	Sirach 37-38	Amos 1-2
21	Sirach 39-40	Amos 3-4
22	Sirach 41-42	Amos 5-6
23	Sirach 43-44	Amos 7-8
24	Sirach 45-46	Amos 9
25	Sirach 47-48	Hosea 1-2
26	Sirach 49-50	Hosea 3-4
27	Sirach 51	Hosea 5-6
28	Tobit 1-3:6	Hosea 7-8
29	Tobit 3:7-4:21	Hosea 9-10
30	Tobit 5-6	Hosea 11-12
31	Tobit 7-8	Hosea 13-14

APRIL

Date	Year 1	Year 2
1	Tobit 9-10	Isaiah 1-2
2	Tobit 11-12	Isaiah 3-4
3	Tobit 13-14	Isaiah 5-6
4	Jonah 1-2	Isaiah 7-8
5	Jonah 3-4	Isaiah 9-10
6	Joel 1-2	Isaiah 11-12
7	Joel 3-4	Isaiah 13-14
8	Nahum 1-2	Isaiah 15-16
9	Nahum 3	Isaiah 17-18
10	Malachi 1-2	Isaiah 19-20
11	Malachi 3	Isaiah 21-22
12	Exodus 1-2	Isaiah 23-24
13	Exodus 3-4	Isaiah 25-26
14	Exodus 5-6	Isaiah 27-28
15	Exodus 7-8	Isaiah 29-30
16	Exodus 9-10	Isaiah 31-32
17	Exodus 11-12	Isaiah 33-34
18	Exodus 13-14	Isaiah 35-36
19	Exodus 15-16	Isaiah 37-38
20	Exodus 17-18	Isaiah 39-40
21	Exodus 19-20	Isaiah 41-42
22	Exodus 21-22	Isaiah 43-44
23	Exodus 23-24	Isaiah 45-46
24	Exodus 25-26	Isaiah 47-48
25	Exodus 27-28	Isaiah 49-50

Date	Year 1	Year 2
26	Exodus 29-30	Isaiah 51-52
27	Exodus 31-32	Isaiah 53-54
28	Exodus 33-34	Isaiah 55-56
29	Exodus 35-36	Isaiah 57-58
30	Exodus 37-38	Isaiah 59-60

MAY

Date	Year 1	Year 2
1	Exodus 39-40	Isaiah 61-62
2	Zephaniah 1-2	Isaiah 63-64
3	Zephaniah 3	Isaiah 65-66
4	Acts 1	Matthew 1
5	Acts 2	Matthew 2
6	Acts 3	Matthew 3
7	Acts 4	Matthew 4
8	Acts 5	Matthew 5
9	Acts 6	Matthew 6
10	Acts 7	Matthew 7
11	Acts 8	Matthew 8
12	Acts 9	Matthew 9
13	Acts 10	Matthew 10
14	Acts 11	Matthew 11
15	Acts 12	Matthew 12
16	Acts 13	Matthew 13
17	Acts 14	Matthew 14
18	Acts 15	Matthew 15
19	Acts 16	Matthew 16
20	Acts 17	Matthew 17
21	Acts 18	Matthew 18
22	Acts 19	Matthew 19
23	Acts 20	Matthew 20
24	Acts 21	Matthew 21
25	Acts 22	Matthew 22
26	Acts 23	Matthew 23
27	Acts 24	Matthew 24
28	Acts 25	Matthew 25
29	Acts 26	Matthew 26
30	Acts 27	Matthew 27
31	Acts 28	Matthew 28

JUNE

Date	Year 1	Year 2
1	Psalms 1-5	Jeremiah 1-2
2	Psalms 6-10	Jeremiah 3-4
3	Psalms 11-15	Jeremiah 5-6
4	Psalms 16-20	Jeremiah 7-8
5	Psalms 21-25	Jeremiah 9-10
6	Psalms 26-30	Jeremiah 11-12
7	Psalms 31-35	Jeremiah 13-14
8	Psalms 36-40	Jeremiah 15-16
9	Psalms 41-45	Jeremiah 17-18
10	Psalms 46-50	Jeremiah 19-20
11	Psalms 51-55	Jeremiah 21-22
12	Psalms 56-60	Jeremiah 23-24
13	Psalms 61-65	Jeremiah 25-26
14	Psalms 66-70	Jeremiah 27-28
15	Psalms 71-75	Jeremiah 29-30
16	Psalms 76-80	Jeremiah 31-32
17	Psalms 81-85	Jeremiah 33-34
18	Psalms 86-90	Jeremiah 35-36
19	Psalms 91-95	Jeremiah 37-38
20	Psalms 96-100	Jeremiah 39-40
21	Psalms 101-105	Jeremiah 41-42
22	Psalms 106-110	Jeremiah 43-44
23	Psalms 111-115	Jeremiah 45-46
24	Psalms 116-120	Jeremiah 47-48
25	Psalms 121-125	Jeremiah 49-50
26	Psalms 126-130	Jeremiah 51-52
27	Psalms 131-135	Ezekiel 1-2
28	Psalms 136-140	Ezekiel 3-4
29	Psalms 141-145	Ezekiel 5-6
30	Psalms 146-150	Ezekiel 7-8

JULY

Date	Year 1	Year 2
1	Zechariah 1-2	Ezekiel 9-10
2	Zechariah 3-4	Ezekiel 11-12
3	Zechariah 5-6	Ezekiel 13-14
4	Zechariah 7-8	Ezekiel 15-16
5	Zechariah 9-10	Ezekiel 17-18
6	Zechariah 11-12	Ezekiel 19-20

Date	Year 1	Year 2
7	Zechariah 13-14	Ezekiel 21-22
8	2 Corinthians 1	Ezekiel 23-24
9	2 Corinthians 2	Ezekiel 25-26
10	2 Corinthians 3	Ezekiel 27-28
11	2 Corinthians 4	Ezekiel 29-30
12	2 Corinthians 5	Ezekiel 31-32
13	2 Corinthians 6	Ezekiel 33-34
14	2 Corinthians 7	Ezekiel 35-36
15	2 Corinthians 8	Ezekiel 37-38
16	2 Corinthians 9	Ezekiel 39-40
17	2 Corinthians 10	Song of Songs 1-2
18	2 Corinthians 11	Song of Songs 3-4
19	2 Corinthians 12	Song of Songs 5-6
20	2 Corinthians 13	Song of Songs 7-8
21	Esther A, 1-2	1 Corinthians 1
22	Esther 3, B, 4	1 Corinthians 2
23	Esther C, D, 5	1 Corinthians 3
24	Esther 6, 7, E	1 Corinthians 4
25	Esther 8, 9, 10, F	1 Corinthians 5
26	Micah 1-2	1 Corinthians 6
27	Micah 3-4	1 Corinthians 7
28	Micah 5-6	1 Corinthians 8
29	Micah 7	1 Corinthians 9
30	Obadiah	1 Corinthians 10
31	Nahum 1-2	1 Corinthians 11

AUGUST

Date	Year 1	Year 2
1	Nahum 3	1 Corinthians 12
2	Habbakuk 1-2	1 Corinthians 13
3	Habbakuk 3	1 Corinthians 14
4	Haggai	1 Corinthians 15
5	Leviticus 1-2	Job 1-2
6	Leviticus 3-4	Job 3-4
7	Leviticus 5-6	Job 5-6
8	Leviticus 7-8	Job 7-8
9	Leviticus 9-10	Job 9-10
10	Leviticus 11-12	Job 11-12
11	Leviticus 13-14	Job 13-14
12	Leviticus 15-16	Job 15-16
13	Leviticus 17-18	Job 17-18
14	Leviticus 19-20	Job 19-20

Date	Year 1	Year 2
15	Leviticus 21-22	Job 21-22
16	Leviticus 23-24	Job 23-24
17	Leviticus 25-26	Job 25-26
18	Leviticus 27	Job 27-28
19	Numbers 1-2	Job 29-30
20	Numbers 3-4	Job 31-32
21	Numbers 5-6	Job 33-34
22	Numbers 7-8	Job 35-36
23	Numbers 9-10	Job 37-38
24	Numbers 11-12	Job 39-40
25	Numbers 13-14	Job 41-42
26	Numbers 15-16	1 Chronicles 1-2
27	Numbers 17-18	1 Chronicles 3-4
28	Numbers 19-20	1 Chronicles 5-6
29	Numbers 21-22	1 Chronicles 7-8
30	Numbers 23-24	1 Chronicles 9-10
31	Numbers 25-26	1 Chronicles 11-12

SEPTEMBER

Date	Year 1	Year 2
1	Numbers 27-28	1 Chronicles 13-14
2	Numbers 29-30	1 Chronicles 15-16
3	Numbers 31-32	1 Chronicles 17-18
4	Numbers 33-34	1 Chronicles 19-20
5	Numbers 35-36	1 Chronicles 21-22
6	Deuteronomy 1-2	1 Chronicles 23-24
7	Deuteronomy 3-4	1 Chronicles 25-26
8	Deuteronomy 5-6	1 Chronicles 27-28
9	Deuteronomy 7-8	1 Chronicles 29
10	Deuteronomy 9-10	2 Chronicles 1-2
11	Deuteronomy 11-12	2 Chronicles 3-4
12	Deuteronomy 13-14	2 Chronicles 5-6
13	Deuteronomy 15-16	2 Chronicles 7-8
14	Deuteronomy 17-18	2 Chronicles 9-10
15	Deuteronomy 19-20	2 Chronicles 11-12
16	Deuteronomy 21-22	2 Chronicles 13-14
17	Deuteronomy 23-24	2 Chronicles 15-16
18	Deuteronomy 25-26	2 Chronicles 17-18
19	Deuteronomy 27-28	2 Chronicles 19-20
20	Deuteronomy 29-30	2 Chronicles 21-22
21	Deuteronomy 31-32	2 Chronicles 23-24
22	Deuteronomy 33-34	2 Chronicles 25-26

Date	Year 1	Year 2
23	Joshua 1-2	2 Chronicles 27-28
24	Joshua 3-4	2 Chronicles 29-30
25	Joshua 5-6	2 Chronicles 31-32
26	Joshua 7-8	2 Chronicles 33-34
27	Joshua 9-10	Galatians 1-2
28	Joshua 11-12	Galatians 3
29	Joshua 13-14	Galatians 4
30	Joshua 15-16	Galatians 5-6

OCTOBER

Date	Year 1	Year 2
1	Joshua 17-18	Philippians 1
2	Joshua 19-20	Philippians 2
3	Joshua 21-22	Philippians 3
4	Joshua 23-24	Philippians 4
5	Judges 1-2	Titus 1-2
6	Judges 3-4	Titus 3
7	Judges 5-6	Proverbs 1-2
8	Judges 7-8	Proverbs 3-4
9	Judges 9-10	Proverbs 5-6
10	Judges 11-12	Proverbs 7-8
11	Judges 13-14	Proverbs 9-10
12	Judges 15-16	Proverbs 11-12
13	Judges 17-18	Proverbs 13-14
14	Judges 19-20	Proverbs 15-16
15	Judges 21	Proverbs 17-18
16	Ruth 1-2	Proverbs 19-20
17	Ruth 3-4	Proverbs 21-22
18	1 Thessalonians 1-2	Proverbs 23-24
19	1 Thessalonians 3-4	Proverbs 25-26
20	1 Thessalonians 5	Proverbs 27-28
21	Colossians 1-2	Proverbs 29-30
22	Colossians 3	Proverbs 31
23	Colossians 4	Wisdom 1-2
24	Ephesians 1	Wisdom 3-4
25	Ephesians 2	Wisdom 5-6
26	Ephesians 3-4	Wisdom 7-8
27	Ephesians 5	Wisdom 9-10
28	Ephesians 6	Wisdom 11-12
29	1 Timothy 1	Wisdom 13-14
30	1 Timothy 2	Wisdom 15-16
31	1 Timothy 3-4	Wisdom 17-19

NOVEMBER

Date	Year 1	Year 2
1	1 Timothy 5-6	Judith 1-2
2	Ezra 1-2	Judith 3-4
3	Ezra 3-4	Judith 5-6
4	Ezra 5-6	Judith 7-8
5	Ezra 7-8	Judith 9-10
6	Ezra 9-10	Judith 11-12
7	Nehemiah 1-2	Judith 13-14
8	Nehemiah 3-4	Judith 15-16
9	Nehemiah 5-6	1 Maccabees 1
10	Nehemiah 7-8	1 Maccabees 2
11	Nehemiah 9-10	1 Maccabees 3-4
12	Nehemiah 11-12	1 Maccabees 5-6
13	Nehemiah 13	1 Maccabees 7-8
14	Philemon	1 Maccabees 9-10
15	Jude	1 Maccabees 11-12
16	Baruch 1-2	1 Maccabees 13-14
17	Baruch 3-4	1 Maccabees 15-16
18	Baruch 5-6	2 Maccabees 1-2
19	Romans 1	2 Maccabees 3-4
20	Romans 2	2 Maccabees 5-6
21	Romans 3	2 Maccabees 7
22	Romans 4	2 Maccabees 8-9
23	Romans 5	2 Maccabees 10-11
24	Romans 6	2 Maccabees 12
25	Romans 7	2 Maccabees 13-14
26	Romans 8	2 Maccabees 15
27	Romans 9	Revelation 1-2
28	Romans 10	Revelation 3-4
29	Romans 11	Revelation 5-6
30	Romans 12	Revelation 7-8

DECEMBER

Date	Year 1	Year 2
1	Romans 13	Revelation 9-10
2	Romans 14	Revelation 11-12
3	Romans 15	Revelation 13-14
4	Daniel 1-2	Revelation 15-16
5	Daniel 3-4	Revelation 17-18
6	Daniel 5-6	Revelation 19-20
7	Daniel 7-8	Revelation 21-22

Date	Year 1	Year 2
8	Daniel 9-10	Luke 1
9	Daniel 11-12	Luke 2
10	Daniel 13-14	Luke 3
11	John 1	Luke 4
12	John 2	Luke 5
13	John 3	Luke 6
14	John 4	Luke 7
15	John 5	Luke 8
16	John 6	Luke 9
17	John 7	Luke 10
18	John 8	Luke 11
19	John 9	Luke 12
20	John 10	Luke 13
21	John 11	Luke 14
22	John 12	Luke 15
23	John 13	Luke 16
24	John 14	Luke 17
25	John 15	Luke 18
26	John 16	Luke 19
27	John 17	Luke 20
28	John 18	Luke 21
29	John 19	Luke 22
30	John 20	Luke 23
31	John 21	Luke 24

Part Three

The Three-Year Reading Plan
(The Bible in Three Years.)

Daily Reading Time averages 5-7 minutes. This reading plan is particularly suited to those who are just beginning to read Scripture every day. The short daily readings will help the beginner develop a pattern of regular Scripture reading and study.

JANUARY

Date	Year 1	Year 2	Year 3
1	Genesis 1-2	1 Chronicles 1	Luke 1
2	Genesis 3-4	1 Chronicles 2	Luke 2
3	Genesis 5-6	1 Chronicles 3	Luke 3
4	Genesis 7-8	1 Chronicles 4	Luke 4
5	Genesis 9-10	1 Chronicles 5	Luke 5
6	Genesis 11-12	1 Chronicles 6	Luke 6
7	Genesis 13-14	1 Chronicles 7	Luke 7
8	Genesis 15-16	1 Chronicles 8-9:1	Luke 8
9	Genesis 17-18	1 Chronicles 9:2-44	Luke 9
10	Genesis 19-20	1 Chronicles 10	Luke 10
11	Genesis 21-22	1 Chronicles 11	Luke 11
12	Genesis 23-24	1 Chronicles 12	Luke 12
13	Genesis 25-26	1 Chronicles 13	Luke 13
14	Genesis 27-28	1 Chronicles 14	Luke 14
15	Genesis 29-30	1 Chronicles 15	Luke 15
16	Genesis 31-32	1 Chronicles 16	Luke 16
17	Genesis 33-34	1 Chronicles 17	Luke 17
18	Genesis 35-36	1 Chronicles 18	Luke 18
19	Genesis 37-38	1 Chronicles 19	Luke 19
20	Genesis 39-40	1 Chronicles 20	Luke 20
21	Genesis 41-42	1 Chronicles 21	Luke 21
22	Genesis 43-45	1 Chronicles 22	Luke 22
23	Genesis 46-48	1 Chronicles 23	Luke 23
24	Genesis 49-50	1 Chronicles 24	Luke 24
25	Exodus 1-2	1 Chronicles 25	John 1
26	Exodus 3-4	1 Chronicles 26	John 2
27	Exodus 5-6	1 Chronicles 27	John 3
28	Exodus 7-8	1 Chronicles 28	John 4
29	Exodus 9-10	1 Chronicles 29	John 5
30	Exodus 11-12	2 Chronicles 1	John 6
31	Exodus 13-14	2 Chronicles 2	John 7

FEBRUARY

Date	Year 1	Year 2	Year 3
1	Exodus 15-16	2 Chronicles 3	John 8
2	Exodus 17-18	2 Chronicles 4	John 9
3	Exodus 19-20	2 Chronicles 5	John 10
4	Exodus 21-22	2 Chronicles 6	John 11
5	Exodus 23-24	2 Chronicles 7	John 12
6	Exodus 25-26	2 Chronicles 8	John 13

Date	Year 1	Year 2	Year 3
7	Exodus 27-28	2 Chronicles 9	John 14
8	Exodus 29-30	2 Chronicles 10	John 15
9	Exodus 31-32	2 Chronicles 11	John 16
10	Exodus 33-34	2 Chronicles 12	John 17
11	Exodus 35-36	2 Chronicles 13	John 18
12	Exodus 37-38	2 Chronicles 14	John 19
13	Exodus 39-40	2 Chronicles 15	John 20
14	Leviticus 1-2	2 Chronicles 16	John 21
15	Leviticus 3-4	2 Chronicles 17	Colossians 1
16	Leviticus 5-6	2 Chronicles 18	Colossians 2
17	Leviticus 7	2 Chronicles 19	Colossians 3
18	Leviticus 8	2 Chronicles 20	Colossians 4
19	Leviticus 9-10	2 Chronicles 21	1 Timothy 1
20	Leviticus 11-12	2 Chronicles 22	1 Timothy 2
21	Leviticus 13-14	2 Chronicles 23	1 Timothy 3
22	Leviticus 15-16	2 Chronicles 24	1 Timothy 4
23	Leviticus 17-18	2 Chronicles 25	1 Timothy 5
24	Leviticus 19-20	2 Chronicles 26	1 Timothy 6
25	Leviticus 21-22	2 Chronicles 27	2 Timothy 1
26	Leviticus 23-24	2 Chronicles 28	2 Timothy 2
27	Leviticus 25-26	2 Chronicles 29	2 Timothy 3
28	Leviticus 27	2 Chronicles 30	2 Timothy 4

MARCH

Date	Year 1	Year 2	Year 3
1	Mark 1	2 Chronicles 31	Psalm 1
2	Mark 2	2 Chronicles 32	Psalm 2
3	Mark 3	2 Chronicles 33	Psalm 3
4	Mark 4	2 Chronicles 34	Psalm 4
5	Mark 5	2 Chronicles 35	Psalm 5
6	Mark 6	2 Chronicles 36	Psalm 6
7	Mark 7	Isaiah 1	Psalm 7
8	Mark 8	Isaiah 2	Psalm 8
9	Acts 1	Isaiah 3-4:1	Psalm 9
10	Acts 2	Isaiah 4:2-6	Psalm 10
11	Acts 3	Isaiah 5	Psalm 11
12	Acts 4	Isaiah 6	Psalm 12
13	Acts 5	Isaiah 7	Psalm 13
14	Acts 6	Isaiah 8:1-22	Psalm 14
15	Acts 7	Isaiah 8:23-9:20	Psalm 15
16	Acts 8	Isaiah 10	Psalm 16

Date	Year 1	Year 2	Year 3
17	Acts 9	Isaiah 11	Psalm 17
18	Acts 10	Isaiah 12	Psalm 18
19	Acts 11	Isaiah 13	Psalm 19
20	Acts 12	Isaiah 14	Psalm 20
21	Acts 13	Isaiah 15	Psalm 21
22	Acts 14	Isaiah 16	Psalm 22
23	Acts 15	Isaiah 17	Psalm 23
24	Acts 16	Isaiah 18	Psalm 24
25	Acts 17	Isaiah 19	Psalm 25
26	Acts 18	Isaiah 20	Psalm 26
27	Acts 19	Isaiah 21	Psalm 27
28	Acts 20	Isaiah 22	Psalm 28
29	Acts 21	Isaiah 23	Psalm 29
30	Acts 22	Isaiah 24	Psalm 30
31	Acts 23	Isaiah 25	Psalm 31

APRIL

Date	Year 1	Year 2	Year 3
1	Acts 24	Isaiah 26	Psalm 32
2	Acts 25	Isaiah 27	Psalm 33
3	Acts 26	Isaiah 28	Psalm 34
4	Acts 27	Isaiah 29	Psalm 35
5	Acts 28	Isaiah 30	Psalm 36
6	Romans 1	Isaiah 31	Psalm 37
7	Romans 2	Isaiah 32	Psalm 38
8	Romans 3	Isaiah 33	Psalm 39
9	Romans 4	Isaiah 34	Psalm 40
10	Romans 5	Isaiah 35	Psalm 41
11	Romans 6	Isaiah 36-37:20	Psalm 42
12	Romans 7	Isaiah 37:21-38	Psalm 43
13	Romans 8	Isaiah 38	Psalm 44
14	Romans 9	Isaiah 39	Psalm 45
15	Romans 10	Isaiah 40	Psalm 46
16	Romans 11	Isaiah 41	Psalm 47
17	Romans 12	Isaiah 42	Psalm 48
18	Romans 13	Isaiah 43	Psalm 49
19	Romans 14	Isaiah 44	Psalm 50
20	Romans 15	Isaiah 45	Psalm 51
21	Romans 16	Isaiah 46	Psalm 52
22	1 Corinthians 1	Isaiah 47	Psalm 53
23	1 Corinthians 2	Isaiah 48	Psalm 54
24	1 Corinthians 3	Isaiah 49	Psalm 55

Date	Year 1	Year 2	Year 3
25	1 Corinthians 4	Isaiah 50	Psalm 56
26	1 Corinthians 5	Isaiah 51	Psalm 57
27	1 Corinthians 6	Isaiah 52	Psalm 58
28	1 Corinthians 7	Isaiah 53	Psalm 59
29	1 Samuel 1	Isaiah 54	Psalm 60
30	1 Samuel 2	Isaiah 55	Psalm 61

MAY

Date	Year 1	Year 2	Year 3
1	1 Samuel 3-4	Zechariah 1	Psalm 62
2	1 Samuel 5-7:1	Zechariah 2	Psalm 63
3	1 Samuel 7:2-8:22	Zechariah 3	Psalm 64
4	1 Samuel 9-10	Zechariah 4	Psalm 65
5	1 Samuel 11-12	Zechariah 5	Psalm 66
6	1 Samuel 13-14	Zechariah 6	Psalm 67
7	1 Samuel 15-16	Zechariah 7	Psalm 68
8	1 Samuel 17-18	Zechariah 8	Psalm 69
9	1 Samuel 19-21:1	Zechariah 9	Psalm 70
10	1 Samuel 21:2-22:23	Zechariah 10	Psalm 71
11	1 Samuel 23-25:1	Zechariah 11	Psalm 72
12	1 Samuel 25:2-26:25	Zechariah 12	Psalm 73
13	1 Samuel 27-28	Zechariah 13	Psalm 74
14	1 Samuel 29-31	Zechariah 14	Psalm 75
15	2 Samuel 1-3:1	Malachi 1-2	Psalm 76
16	2 Samuel 3:2-4:12	Malachi 3	Psalm 77
17	2 Samuel 5-6	Matthew 1	Psalm 78
18	2 Samuel 7-8	Matthew 2	Psalm 79
19	2 Samuel 9-10	Matthew 3	Psalm 80
20	2 Samuel 11-12	Matthew 4	Psalm 81
21	2 Samuel 13-14	Matthew 5	Psalm 82-83
22	2 Samuel 15-16:22	Matthew 6	Psalm 84
23	2 Samuel 16:23-19:1	Matthew 7	Psalm 85
24	2 Samuel 19:2-20:26	Matthew 8	Psalm 86
25	2 Samuel 21-22	Matthew 9	Psalm 87
26	2 Samuel 23-24	Matthew 10	Psalm 88
27	1 Kings 1-2	Matthew 11	Psalm 89
28	1 Kings 3-5:14	Matthew 12	Psalm 90
29	1 Kings 5:15-6:38	Matthew 13	Psalm 91
30	1 Kings 7-8	Matthew 14	Psalm 92
31	1 Kings 9-10	Matthew 15	Psalm 93-94

JUNE

Date	Year 1	Year 2	Year 3
1	1 Kings 11-12	Matthew 16	Psalm 95-96
2	1 Kings 13-14	Matthew 17	Psalm 97-98
3	1 Kings 15-16	Matthew 18	Psalm 99-100
4	1 Kings 17-18	Matthew 19	Psalm 101
5	1 Kings 19-20	Matthew 20	Psalm 102
6	1 Kings 21-22	Matthew 21	Psalm 103
7	2 Kings 1-2	Matthew 22	Psalm 104
8	2 Kings 3-4	Matthew 23	Psalm 105
9	2 Kings 5-6	Matthew 24	Psalm 106
10	2 Kings 7-8	Matthew 25	Psalm 107
11	2 Kings 9-10	Matthew 26-27:2	Psalm 108
12	2 Kings 11-12	Matthew 27:3-66	Proverbs 1
13	2 Kings 13-14	Matthew 28	Proverbs 2
14	2 Kings 15-16	Galatians 1	Proverbs 3
15	2 Kings 17-18	Galatians 2	Proverbs 4
16	2 Kings 19-20	Galatians 3	Proverbs 5
17	2 Kings 21-22	Galatians 4	Proverbs 6
18	2 Kings 23-24:17	Galatians 5	Proverbs 7
19	2 Kings 24:18-25:30	Galatians 6	Proverbs 8
20	Ezra 1-2	Ephesians 1	Proverbs 9
21	Ezra 3-4	Ephesians 2	Proverbs 10
22	Ezra 5-6	Ephesians 3	Proverbs 11
23	Ezra 7-8	Ephesians 4	Proverbs 12
24	Ezra 9-10	Ephesians 5	Proverbs 13
25	Nehemiah 1-2	Ephesians 6	Proverbs 14
26	Nehemiah 3-4	1 John 1	Proverbs 15
27	Nehemiah 5-6	1 John 2	Proverbs 16
28	Nehemiah 7-8	1 John 3	Proverbs 17
29	Nehemiah 9-10	1 John 4	Proverbs 18
30	Nehemiah 11-12	1 John 5	Proverbs 19

JULY

Date	Year 1	Year 2	Year 3
1	Nehemiah 13	Isaiah 56	Proverbs 20
2	Tobit 1-2	Isaiah 57	Proverbs 21
3	Tobit 3-4	Lamentations 1	Proverbs 22
4	Tobit 5-6	Lamentations 2	Proverbs 23
5	Tobit 7-8	Lamentations 3	Proverbs 24
6	Tobit 9-10	Lamentations 4	Proverbs 25

Date	Year 1	Year 2	Year 3
7	Tobit 11-12	Lamentations 5	Proverbs 26
8	Tobit 13-14	Baruch 1-2:10	Proverbs 27
9	Judith 1-2	Baruch 2:11-2:35	Proverbs 28
10	Judith 3-4	Baruch 3-4:4	Proverbs 29
11	Judith 5-6	Baruch 4:5-5	Proverbs 30
12	Judith 7-8	Baruch 6	Proverbs 31
13	Judith 9-10:20	Ezekiel 1	Ecclesiastes 1
14	Judith 10:21-12:20	Ezekiel 2	Ecclesiastes 2
15	Judith 13-15:3	Ezekiel 3	Ecclesiastes 3
16	Judith 15:4-16:25	Ezekiel 4	Ecclesiastes 4
17	Esther A, 1-2	Ezekiel 5	Ecclesiastes 5
18	Esther 3, B, 4	Ezekiel 6	Ecclesiastes 6
19	Esther C, D	Ezekiel 7	Ecclesiastes 7
20	Esther 5-7	Ezekiel 8	Ecclesiastes 8
21	Esther 8, E	Ezekiel 9	Ecclesiastes 9
22	Esther 9, F	Ezekiel 10	Ecclesiastes 10
23	1 Maccabees 1	Ezekiel 11	Ecclesiastes 11
24	1 Maccabees 2	Ezekiel 12	Ecclesiastes 12
25	1 Maccabees 3	Ezekiel 13	Song of Songs 1
26	1 Maccabees 4	Ezekiel 14	Song of Songs 2
27	1 Maccabees 5	Ezekiel 15	Song of Songs 3
28	1 Maccabees 6	Ezekiel 16	Song of Songs 4
29	1 Maccabees 7	Ezekiel 17	Song of Songs 5
30	1 Maccabees 8	Ezekiel 18	Song of Songs 6
31	1 Maccabees 9	Ezekiel 19	Song of Songs 7-8

AUGUST

Date	Year 1	Year 2	Year 3
1	1 Maccabees 10	Ezekiel 20	Wisdom 1
2	1 Maccabees 11	Ezekiel 21	Wisdom 2
3	1 Maccabees 12	Ezekiel 22	Wisdom 3
4	1 Maccabees 13	Ezekiel 23	Wisdom 4
5	1 Maccabees 14	Ezekiel 24	Wisdom 5
6	1 Maccabees 15	Ezekiel 25	Wisdom 6
7	1 Maccabees 16	Ezekiel 26	Wisdom 7
8	1 Maccabees 17	Ezekiel 27	Wisdom 8
9	2 Maccabees 1	Ezekiel 28	Wisdom 9
10	2 Maccabees 2	Ezekiel 29	Wisdom 10
11	2 Maccabees 3	Ezekiel 30	Wisdom 11
12	2 Maccabees 4	Ezekiel 31	Wisdom 12
13	2 Maccabees 5	Ezekiel 32	Wisdom 13
14	2 Maccabees 6	Ezekiel 33	Wisdom 14

Date	Year 1	Year 2	Year 3
15	2 Maccabees 7	Ezekiel 34	Wisdom 15
16	2 Maccabees 8	Ezekiel 35	Wisdom 16
17	2 Maccabees 9	Ezekiel 36	Wisdom 17
18	2 Maccabees 10	Ezekiel 37	Wisdom 18
19	2 Maccabees 11	Ezekiel 38	Wisdom 19
20	2 Maccabees 12	Ezekiel 39	Sirach 1
21	2 Maccabees 13	Ezekiel 40	Sirach 2
22	2 Maccabees 14	Ezekiel 41	Sirach 3
23	2 Maccabees 15	Ezekiel 42	Sirach 4
24	Mark 9	Ezekiel 43	Sirach 5
25	Mark 10	Ezekiel 44	Sirach 6
26	Mark 11	Ezekiel 45	Sirach 7
27	Mark 12	Ezekiel 46	Sirach 8
28	Mark 13	Ezekiel 47	Sirach 9
29	Mark 14	Ezekiel 48	Sirach 10
30	Mark 15	Daniel 1	Sirach 11
31	Mark 16	Daniel 2	Sirach 12

SEPTEMBER

Date	Year 1	Year 2	Year 3
1	Numbers 1-2	Daniel 3	Sirach 13
2	Numbers 3-4	Daniel 4	Sirach 14
3	Numbers 5-6	Daniel 5-6:1	Sirach 15
4	Numbers 7-8	Daniel 6:2-49	Sirach 16
5	Numbers 9-10	Daniel 7	Sirach 17
6	Numbers 11-12	Daniel 8	Sirach 18
7	Numbers 13-14	Daniel 9	Sirach 19
8	Numbers 15-16	Daniel 10	Sirach 20
9	Numbers 17-18	Daniel 11	Sirach 21
10	Numbers 19-20	Daniel 12	Sirach 22
11	Numbers 21-22:40	Daniel 13	Sirach 23
12	Numbers 22:41-24:25	Daniel 14	Sirach 24
13	Numbers 25-26	Hosea 1	Sirach 25
14	Numbers 27-28	Hosea 2	Sirach 26
15	Numbers 29-30	Hosea 3	Sirach 27
16	Numbers 31-32	Hosea 4	Sirach 28
17	Numbers 33-34	Hosea 5	Sirach 29
18	Numbers 35-36	Hosea 6	Sirach 30
19	Deuteronomy 1-2	Hosea 7	Sirach 31
20	Deuteronomy 3-4	Hosea 8	Sirach 32
21	Deuteronomy 5-6	Hosea 9	Sirach 33
22	Deuteronomy 7-8	Hosea 10	Sirach 34

Date	Year 1	Year 2	Year 3
23	Deuteronomy 9-10	Hosea 11	Sirach 35
24	Deuteronomy 11-12	Hosea 12	Sirach 36
25	Deuteronomy 13-14	Hosea 13-14:1	Sirach 37
26	Deuteronomy 15-16:20	Hosea 14:2-10	Sirach 38
27	Deuteronomy 16:21-18:22	Joel 1	Sirach 39
28	Deuteronomy 19-20	Joel 2	Sirach 40
29	Deuteronomy 21-22	Joel 3	Sirach 41
30	Deuteronomy 23-25:4	Joel 4	Sirach 42

OCTOBER

Date	Year 1	Year 2	Year 3
1	Deuteronomy 25:5-26:19	Amos 1	Sirach 43
2	Deuteronomy 27-28	Amos 2	Sirach 44
3	Deuteronomy 29-30	Amos 3	Sirach 45
4	Deuteronomy 31-32	Amos 4	Sirach 46
5	Deuteronomy 33-34	Amos 5	Sirach 47
6	Joshua 1-2	Amos 6	Sirach 48
7	Joshua 3-4	Amos 7	Sirach 49
8	Joshua 5-6	Amos 8	Sirach 50
9	Joshua 7-8	Amos 9	Sirach 51
10	Joshua 9-10	Obadiah 1	Psalm 109
11	Joshua 11-12	Obadiah 2	Psalm 110-111
12	Joshua 13-14	Jonah 1-2	Psalm 112-114
13	Joshua 15-16	Jonah 3-4	Psalm 115-116
14	Joshua 17-18	Micah 1	Psalm 117-118
15	Joshua 19-20	Micah 2	Psalm 119:1-88
16	Joshua 21-22	Micah 3	Psalm 119:89-176
17	Joshua 23-24	Micah 4	Psalm 120-121
18	Judges 1-2	Micah 5	Psalm 122-124
19	Judges 3-4	Micah 6	Psalm 125-126
20	Judges 5-6	Micah 7	Psalm 127-128
21	Judges 7-8	Nahum 1-2	Psalm 129-132
22	Judges 9-10	Nahum 3	Psalm 133-135
23	Judges 11-12	Habakkuk 1-2:1	Psalm 136
24	Judges 13-14	Habakkuk 2:2-20	Psalm 137-138
25	Judges 15	Habakkuk 3	Psalm 139
26	Judges 16-17	Zephaniah 1	Psalm 140
27	Judges 18-19	Zephaniah 2	Psalm 141
28	Judges 20-21	Zephaniah 3	Psalm 142-143
29	Ruth 1-2	Haggai 1	Psalm 144
30	Ruth 3-4	Haggai 2:1-9	Psalm 145
31	1 Corinthians 8-9	Haggai 2:10-23	Psalm 146

NOVEMBER

Date	Year 1	Year 2	Year 3
1	1 Corinthians 10	Isaiah 58	Psalm 147
2	1 Corinthians 11	Isaiah 59	Psalm 148
3	1 Corinthians 12:1-11a	Isaiah 60	Psalm 149
4	1 Corinthians 12:11b-13	Isaiah 61	Psalm 150
5	1 Corinthians 14	Isaiah 62	Job 1
6	1 Corinthians 15	Isaiah 63	Job 2
7	1 Corinthians 16	Isaiah 64	Job 3
8	2 Corinthians 1	Isaiah 65	Job 4-5
9	2 Corinthians 2	Isaiah 66	Job 6-7
10	2 Corinthians 3	Jeremiah 1	Job 8
11	2 Corinthians 4	Jeremiah 2	Job 9-10
12	2 Corinthians 5	Jeremiah 3	Job 11
13	2 Corinthians 6	Jeremiah 4	Job 12-13
14	2 Corinthians 7	Jeremiah 5	Job 14
15	2 Corinthians 8	Jeremiah 6	Job 15
16	2 Corinthians 9	Jeremiah 7	Job 16-17
17	2 Corinthians 10	Jeremiah 8	Job 18
18	2 Corinthians 11	Jeremiah 9	Job 19
19	2 Corinthians 12	Jeremiah 10	Job 20
20	2 Corinthians 13	Jeremiah 11	Job 21
21	Philippians 1	Jeremiah 12	Job 22
22	Philippians 2	Jeremiah 13	Job 23-24
23	Philippians 3	Jeremiah 14	Job 25-27
24	Philippians 4	Jeremiah 15	Job 28
25	Hebrews 1	Jeremiah 16	Job 29
26	Hebrews 2	Jeremiah 17	Job 30
27	Hebrews 3	Jeremiah 18	Job 31
28	Hebrews 4	Jeremiah 19	Job 32
29	Hebrews 5	Jeremiah 20	Job 33
30	Hebrews 6	Jeremiah 21	Job 34

DECEMBER

Date	Year 1	Year 2	Year 3
1	Hebrews 7	Jeremiah 22	Job 35-36
2	Hebrews 8	Jeremiah 23	Job 37
3	Hebrews 9	Jeremiah 24	Job 38
4	Hebrews 10	Jeremiah 25	Job 39
5	Hebrews 11	Jeremiah 26	Job 40
6	Hebrews 12	Jeremiah 27	Job 41
7	Hebrews 13	Jeremiah 28	Job 42

Date	Year 1	Year 2	Year 3
8	Titus 1	Jeremiah 29	Philemon
9	Titus 2	Jeremiah 30	1 Peter 1
10	Titus 3	Jeremiah 31	1 Peter 2
11	Revelation 1	Jeremiah 32	1 Peter 3
12	Revelation 2	Jeremiah 33	1 Peter 4
13	Revelation 3	Jeremiah 34	1 Peter 5
14	Revelation 4	Jeremiah 35	2 Peter 1
15	Revelation 5	Jeremiah 36	2 Peter 2
16	Revelation 6	Jeremiah 37	2 Peter 3
17	Revelation 7	Jeremiah 38	James 1
18	Revelation 8	Jeremiah 39	James 2
19	Revelation 9	Jeremiah 40	James 3
20	Revelation 10	Jeremiah 41	James 4
21	Revelation 11	Jeremiah 42	James 5
22	Revelation 12	Jeremiah 43	1 Thessalonians 1
23	Revelation 13	Jeremiah 44	1 Thessalonians 2
24	Revelation 14	Jeremiah 45	1 Thessalonians 3
25	Revelation 15-16	Jeremiah 46	1 Thessalonians 4
26	Revelation 17	Jeremiah 47	1 Thessalonians 5
27	Revelation 18	Jeremiah 48	2 Thessalonians 1
28	Revelation 19	Jeremiah 49	2 Thessalonians 2
29	Revelation 20	Jeremiah 50	2 Thessalonians 3
30	Revelation 21	Jeremiah 51	Jude
31	Revelation 22	Jeremiah 52	2 John and 3 John

Part Four

Additional Scripture Readings for the Special Liturgical Seasons of the Church Year

(Seasonal Readings for Advent, Christmas, Lent, and Easter)

These readings for the liturgical seasons can be profitably used with any of the three reading plans during the church year. But there will occasionally be some overlap with the readings covered by all three plans, particularly with the two-year plan, since that plan is keyed to the daily readings of the liturgical year.

ADVENT

Day	Readings
1st Sunday of Advent	Jeremiah 33:14-6; 1 Thessalonians 3:12-4:2; Luke 21:25-28, 34-36
Monday:	Isaiah 2:1-5 (For cycle B & C) or Is 4:2-6 (For cycle A); Matthew 8:5-11
Tuesday:	Isaiah 11:1-10; Luke 10:21-24
Wednesday:	Isaiah 25:6-10; Matthew 15:29-37
Thursday:	Isaiah 26:1-6; Matthew 7:21, 24-27
Friday:	Isaiah 29:17-24; Matthew 9:27-31
Saturday:	Isaiah 30:19-21, 23-26; Matthew 9:35-10:1, 6-8
2nd Sunday of Advent	Isaiah 40:1-5, 9-11; 2 Peter 3:8-14; Mark 1:1-8
Monday:	Isaiah 35:1-10; Luke 5:17-26
Tuesday:	Isaiah 40:1-11; Matthew 18:12-14
Wednesday:	Isaiah 40:25-31; Matthew 11:28-30
Thursday:	Isaiah 41:13-20; Matthew 11:11-15
Friday:	Isaiah 48:17-19; Matthew 11:16-19
Saturday:	Isaiah 48:1-4, 9-11; Matthew 17:10-13
3rd Sunday of Advent	Isaiah 61:1-2, 10-11; James 5:7-10; Matthew 11:2-11
Monday:	Numbers 24:2-7, 15-17; Matthew 21:23-27
Tuesday:	Zephaniah 3:1-2, 13-20; Matthew 21:28-32
Wednesday:	Isaiah 45:6-8, 18, 21-25; Luke 7:18-23
Thursday:	Isaiah 54:1-10; Luke 7:24-30
Friday:	Isaiah 56:1-3, 6-8; John 5:33-36
Saturday:	Genesis 49:2, 8-10; Matthew 1:1-17
4th Sunday of Advent	2 Samuel 7:1-16; Romans 16:25-27; Luke 1:26-38
Monday:	Judges 13:2-7, 24-25; Luke 1:5-25
Tuesday:	Isaiah 7:10-14; Luke 1:26-38
Wednesday:	Song of Songs 2:8-14 (or Zephaniah 3:14-18); Luke 1:39-45
Thursday:	1 Samuel 1:24-28; Luke 1:46-56
Friday:	Malachi 3:1-4, 23-24; Luke 1:57-66
Saturday:	2 Samuel 7:1-5, 8-11, 16; Luke 1:67-79

CHRISTMAS

Day	Readings
Midnight:	Isaiah 9:1-6; Titus 2:11-14; Luke 2:1-14
Dawn:	Isaiah 62:11-12; Titus 3:4-7; Luke 2:15-20
Christmas Day:	Isaiah 62:7-10; Hebrews 1:1-6; John 1:1-18 (or 1:1-5, 9-14)

Day	Readings
Octave of Christmas	
Dec. 26:	Acts 6:8-10; 7:54-59; Matthew 10:17-22
Dec. 27:	1 John 1:1-4; John 20:2-8
Dec. 28:	1 John 1:5-2:2; Matthew 2:13-18
Dec. 29:	1 John 2:3-11; Luke 2:22-35
Dec. 30:	John 2:12-17; Luke 2:36-40
Holy Family	Sirach 3:2-6; 12-14; Col 3:12-21; If year A: Matthew 2:13-15, 19-23; If year B: Luke 2:22-40 or 2:22, 39-40; If year C: Luke 2:41-52 Dec. 31: 1 John 2:18-21; John 1:1-18
Solemnity of Our Lady	Numbers 6:22-27; Galatians 4:4-7; Luke 2:16-21
Day 2:	1 John 2:22-28; John 1:19-28
Day 3:	1 John 2:29-3:6; John 1:29-34
Day 4:	1 John 3:7-10; John 2:35-42
Day 5:	1 John 3:11-21; John 1:43-51
Day 6:	1 John 5:5-13; Mark 1:7-11
Day 7:	1 John 5:14-21; John 2:1-12
Epiphany	Isaiah 60:1-6; Ephesians 3:2-6; Matthew 2:1-12
Day 2:	1 John 3:22-4:6; Matthew 4:12-17, 23-25
Day 3:	1 John 4:7-10; Mark 6:34-44
Day 4:	1 John 4:11-18; Mark 6:45-52
Day 5:	1 John 4:19-5:4; Luke 4:14-22
Day 6:	1 John 5:5-13; Luke 5:12-16
Day 7:	1 John 5:14-21; John 3:22-30
Baptism of our Lord:	Isaiah 42:1-4, 6-7; Acts 10:34-38; Mark 1:7-12

LENT

Day	Readings
Ash Wednesday	Joel 2:12-18; 2 Corinthians 5:20-6:2; Matthew 6:1-6, 16-18
Thursday:	Deuteronomy 30:15-20; Luke 9:22-25
Friday:	Isaiah 58:1-9; Matthew 9:14-15
Saturday:	Isaiah 58:9-14; Luke 5:27-32
1st Sunday of Lent	Genesis 9:8-15; 1 Peter 3:18-22; Mark 1:12-15
Monday:	Leviticus 19:1-2; 11-18; Matthew 25:31-46
Tuesday:	Isaiah 55:10-11; Matthew 6:7-15
Wednesday:	Jonah 3:1-10; Luke 11:29-32
Thursday:	Esther C:12, 14-16, 23-25; Matthew 7:7-12
Friday:	Ezekiel 18:21-28; Matthew 5:20-26
Saturday:	Deuteronomy 26:16-19; Matthew 5:43-48

Day	Readings
2nd Sunday of Lent	Genesis 22:1-2, 9, 10-13, 15-18; Romans 8:31-34; Mark 9:2-10
Monday:	Daniel 9:4-10; Luke 6:36-38
Tuesday:	Isaiah 1:10, 16-20; Matthew 23:1-12
Wednesday:	Jeremiah 18:18-20; Matthew 20:17-28
Thursday:	Jeremiah 17:5-10; Luke 16:19-31
Friday:	Genesis 37:3-4, 12-13, 17-28; Matthew 21:33-43, 45-46
Saturday:	Micah 7:14-15, 18-20; Luke 15:1-3, 11-32
3rd Sunday of Lent	Exodus 20:1-17 (or 20:1-3, 7-8, 12-17); 1 Corinthians 2:22-25; John 2:13-25
Monday:	2 Kings 5:1-15; Luke 4:24-30
Tuesday:	Daniel 3:25, 34-43; Matthew 18:21-35
Wednesday:	Deuteronomy 4:1, 5-9; Matthew 5:17-19
Thursday:	Jeremiah 7:23-28; Luke 11:14-23
Friday:	Hosea 14:2-10; Mark 12:28-34
Saturday:	Hosea 6:1-6; Luke 18:9-14
4th Sunday of Lent	2 Chronicles 36:14-17, 19-23; Ephesians 2:4-10; John 3:14-21
Monday:	Isaiah 65:17-21; John 4:43-54
Tuesday:	Ezekiel 47:1-9, 12; John 5:1-3, 5-16
Wednesday:	Isaiah 49:8-15; John 5:17-30
Thursday:	Exodus 32:7-14; John 5:31-47
Friday:	Wisdom 2:1, 12-22; John 7:1-2, 10, 25-30
Saturday:	Jeremiah 11:18-20; John 7:40-53
5th Sunday of Lent	Jeremiah 31:31-34; Hebrews 5:7-9; John 12:20-33
Monday:	Daniel 13:1-9, 15-17, 19-30, 33-62 (or 13:41-62); John 8:1-11 (or John 8:12-20 if year C)
Tuesday:	Numbers 21:4-9; John 8:21-30
Wednesday:	Daniel 3:14-20, Psalms 91-92, 95; John 8:31-42
Thursday:	Genesis 17:3-9; John 8:51-59
Friday:	Jeremiah 20:10-13; John 10:31-42
Saturday:	Ezekiel 37:21-28; John 11:45-57
Passion/Palm Sunday	Isaiah 50:4-7; Philippians 2:6-11; Mark 14:1-15, 47 (or 15:1-39)
Monday:	Isaiah 42:1-7; John 12:1-11
Tuesday:	Isaiah 49:1-6; John 13:21-33, 36-38
Wednesday:	Isaiah 50:4-9; Matthew 26:14-25
Holy Thursday:	Isaiah 61:1-3, 6, 8-9; Revelation 1:5-8; Luke 22:1-38
Good Friday:	Isaiah 52:13-53:12; Matthew 26-27:56; Luke 22-23:49
Holy Saturday:	Jonah 2; Matthew 27:57-66; Luke 23:50-56

EASTER

Day	Readings
Easter Sunday	Acts 10:34, 37-43; Colossians 3:1-4 or 1 Corinthians 5:6-8; John 20:1-9 (or Mark 16:1-8 or Luke 24:13-35)

Octave of Easter
Monday: Acts 2:14, 22-32; Matthew 28:8-15
Tuesday: Acts 2:36-41; John 20:11-18
Wednesday: Acts 3:1-10; Luke 24:13-35
Thursday: Acts 3:11-26; Luke 24:35-48
Friday: Acts 4:1-12; John 21:1-14
Saturday: Acts 4:13-21; Mark 16:9-15

2nd Sunday of Easter Acts 2:42-47; 1 Peter 1:3-9; John 20:19-31
Monday: Acts 4:23-31; John 3:1-8
Tuesday: Acts 4:32-37; John 3:7-15
Wednesday: Acts 5:17-26; John 3:16-21
Thursday: Acts 5:27-33; John 3:31-36
Friday: Acts 5:34-42; John 6:1-15
Saturday: Acts 6:1-7; John 6:16-21

3rd Sunday of Easter Acts 2:14, 22-28; 1 Peter 1:17-21; Luke 24:13-35
Monday: Acts 6:8-15; John 6:22-29
Tuesday: Acts 7:51-8:1; John 6:30-35
Wednesday: Acts 8:1-8; John 6:35-40
Thursday: Acts 8:26-40; John 6:44-51
Friday: Acts 9:1-20; John 6:52-59
Saturday: Acts 9:31-42; John 6:60-69

4th Sunday of Easter Acts 2:14a, 36-41; 1 Peter 2:20b-25; John 10:1-10
Monday: Acts 11:1-18; John 10:1-10 (In year A, John 10:11-18)
Tuesday: Acts 11:19-26; John 10:22-30
Wednesday: Acts 12:24-13:5; John 12:44-50
Thursday: Acts 13:13-25; John 13:16-20
Friday: Acts 13:26-33; John 14:1-6
Saturday: Acts 13:44-52; John 14:7-14

5th Sunday of Easter Acts 6:1-7; 1 Peter 2:4-9; John 14:1-12
Monday: Acts 14:5-18; John 14:21-26
Tuesday: Acts 14:19-28; John 14:27-31
Wednesday: Acts 15:1-6; John 15:1-8
Thursday: Acts 15:7-21; John 15:9-11
Friday: Acts 15:22-31; John 15:12-17
Saturday: Acts 16:1-10; John 15:18-21

6th Sunday of Easter Acts 8:5-8, 14-17; 1 Peter 3:15-18; John 14:15-21

Day	Readings
Monday:	Acts 16:11-15; John 15:26-16:4
Tuesday:	Acts 16:22-34; John 16:5-11
Wednesday:	Acts 17:15, 22-18:1; John 16:12-15
Ascension Thursday	Acts 1:1-11; Ephesians 1:17-23; Mark 16:15-20
Friday:	Acts 18:9-18; John 16:20-23
Saturday:	Acts 18:23-28; John 16:23-28
7th Sunday of Easter	Acts 1:12-14; 1 Peter 4:13-16; John 17:1-11a
Monday:	Acts 19:1-8; John 16:29-33
Tuesday:	Acts 20:17-27; John 17:1-11
Wednesday:	Acts 20:28-38; John 17:11-19
Thursday:	Acts 22:30; 23:6-11; John 17:20-26
Friday:	Acts 25:13-21; John 21:15-19
Saturday:	Acts 28:16-20, 30-31; John 21:20-25
Pentecost	Acts 2:1-11; 1 Corinthians 12:3-7, 12-13; John 20:19-23